American Quilter
WITHDRAWN
Damaged, Obsolete, or Surplus
Jackson County Library Services

D0506244

American Quilter

with $\mathcal{J}eanna$ $\mathcal{J}uleson$

Tips, Techniques & Lifestyles

JACKSON COUNTY LIBRARY SERVICES
MEDFORD, OREGON 97501

Located in Paducah, Kentucky, the American Quilter's Society (AQS) is dedicated to promoting the accomplishments of today's quilters. Through its publications and events, AQS strives to honor today's quilt-makers and their work and to inspire future creativity and innovation in quiltmaking.

EDITOR: JAY STATEN
COPY EDITOR: BARBARA SMITH
GRAPHIC DESIGN: AMY CHASE
COVER DESIGN: MICHAEL BUCKINGHAM

Library of Congress Cataloging-in-Publication Data
On File

Additional copies of this book may be ordered from the American Quilter's Society, PO Box 3290, Paducah, KY 42002-3290, or call 1-800-626-5420 or online at www.AmericanQuilter.com.

Copyright © 2005, Jeanna Juleson

All rights reserved. No part of this book may be reproduced, stored in any retrieval system, or transmitted in any form, or by any means including but not limited to electronic, mechanical, photocopy, recording, or otherwise, without the written consent of the author and publisher.

Table of Contents

New Frontier

"So, what do you know about television?" That's how it started—that simple! Meredith Schroeder, executive producer of *American Quilter*, was doing what she always does for the American Quilter's Society. She asks probing questions on interesting topics.

That question began a chain of events that propelled AQS into a new world of lights, camera, action. The truth is, we didn't know much about television in the spring of 2003. So the first thing we needed to do was learn about it. Off we went to the television industry trade shows to talk to television producers, executives, agents, buyers, and just about anyone who could give us information.

After three months of research, we had accumulated a wealth of facts, figures, hearsay, and assumptions. Everything pointed to a simple fact that it was time for the American Quilter's Society to take an evolutionary leap into television.

THE IDEA

American Quilter was conceived that spring. We wanted a fresh, contemporary show that was focused on the lives of today's quilters and less oriented to technique and quilting. In one of the many meetings, someone suggested, "We want to be the *National Geographic* of quilting."

The American Quilter's Society knows about the passion of today's quilter. For twenty years, the AQS staff has been in the enviable position of working daily with quilters through our books, quilt shows, contests, *American Quilter* magazine, and the constant contact with our members. The laughter, dedication, community, language, and most of all, art, of these dedicated women and men formed the foundation of AQS, and they would be the foundation of the new television show.

That's it! *American Quilter* is a magazine-style television show that focuses on the experiences of rich and diverse lifestyles. We would travel the length and breadth of the continent and beyond, to cover all aspects of this fascinating world. We would look at quilts, of course. We would visit top quilters in their studios and learn about quilting from experts. Interesting quilting events would keep us on the road to new and exciting places.

THE CREW

But first, we had to get a production crew and make a pilot. Our many informed sources had been brutally frank about having a good pilot episode, "None of the networks are going to give you the time of day unless they see a good pilot first," advised one of the top public relations people in the United States. "Make a good pilot, show your stuff, and you'll get placement."

Through a series of events triggered by our attendance at the television conventions, we were introduced to Curt Worden and Gloria Bailen of Context Media. This dynamite duo came with a wealth of experience in television and documentary film. They have worked with the likes of Tom Brokaw, Barbara Walters, Martha Stewart, and Ted Koppel. But were they ready for quilts?

Curt and Gloria maintained a warm, lighthearted, and professional working environment. —JJ

"I think they envisioned quilting of one hundred years ago, when they first met with us," says Jay Staten, associate publisher with AQS. It was spring in Paducah. "Curt and Gloria walked into the Museum of the American Quilter's Society. They took one look around and stopped dead in their tracks." This was definitely not the quilt world they had expected. Ideas about the show and how it should be constructed flew around the table at that first meeting, and Curt and Gloria immediately jumped at the chance to sign onto the project.

Their sense of fun carried through to the film crew, who added their own, often hilarious, moments. After hanging and taking down dozens of magnificent quilts for the various episodes, the crew members decided it was their time for recognition. They had a rather "well-used" sound blanket, which resembles those that a moving company might use to wrap furniture. They proudly hung it on the set, designating it as their own "Quilt of the Week." —JJ

THE STUDIO

The Challenge—find a quilt studio that could be used as a television studio. We wanted the authentic feel of a real working quilt studio. The film crew wanted sixteen-foot ceilings, good sound and light control. The answer— the studios of Marie and Jim Seroskie (also the home of Katie Lane Quilts) of Amherst, New Hampshire.

Always smiling or regaling us with her jokes, Marie takes the stage to film her commercial for Katie Lane Quilts.

Marie and Jim Seroskie were gracious and generous hosts. For the two weeks of our massive "invasion," we enjoyed the cozy comforts of their gorgeous New Hampshire home. —JJ

A view of the luscious, verdant hillside surrounding the Seroskie home.

The Context Media crew rolled in with their truck full of ladders, cables, booms, and studio equipment. Roger Yergeau, our production manager, took only one day to turn the picturesque New England quilt studio into a modern, state-of-the-art television studio. "There was a great deal of laughter and creativity on the set," says Helen Squire. "It was a real community effort to make the best show possible." In just three days, Context Media had filmed all the footage needed for the pilot episode, and the crew restored Marie's beloved studio to its former glory.

Next stop, the Textile Museum in Washington D.C.—the Blues and Jazz festival was in town, so was the Robert and Helen Cargo collection of quilts. It was smooth jazz and African-American quilts before an enthusiastic audience. The crew spent the day filming with the help of the Textile Museum. Typical of Curt and Gloria's need to delve deeper into the story behind the quilts, they took off for Tuscaloosa, Alabama, to meet with Robert Cargo, in person, at his Folk Art Gallery. After the interview, Robert suggested they interview the Alabama quilters responsible for part of the exhibition. It was yet another look into this fascinating world of quiltmaking.

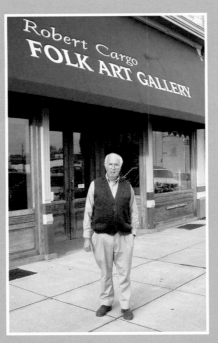

The last part of the show was designed to be a quiet moment—a little time to reflect on the culture of quilting. What better example than a visit to a modern quilt shop located in a charming New England house, circa 1760, that is listed on the National Register of Historic Sites.

Thus concluded our pilot—with it in hand and our agent, Chuck Larsen of October Moon, at our side, we ventured forth into the land of cable television. We entered into negotiations with Lifetime Network, and Lifetime fit our needs perfectly. Before very long, a deal was struck.

American Quilter premiered January 29, 2005, on Lifetime Real Women.

Transforming Marie's quilt studio into a film set.

Jeanna's World

I was correct when I thought I knew a little about quilts. However, as those of us new to the quilting world quickly discover, "We're not in Kansas anymore, Toto!" Since my first step onto the *American Quilter* audition set and my initial meeting with Meredith and Bill Schroeder, my adventures with the American Quilter's Society have opened a world of camaraderie and artistry as boundless as the quilts themselves.

My involvement with AQS began one day in August, when my agent sent me to Nashville to audition for host of a television quilting show. During the subsequent four-hour drive, I reflected on my relationship with quilting and the family ties I have with it. I have enjoyed the sweet comfort of my great-grandmother's quilts since childhood and have become the keeper of almost twenty of my family's treasures. The deep connection I have with my family is alive in the magnificent quilts made by my very dear Mama Osborn. I could not have imagined that my respect and reverence for this art form would lead me into the contemporary world of quilting and art quilts and would begin a new relationship with a long-familiar legacy.

Arriving in Nashville during the 2003 Quilt Exposition, I felt somewhat as though I had landed in "Oz." I marveled at the brilliant, colorful quilt contest entries proudly hanging in rows.

The aisles were alive with excited chatter and flashbulb frenzy. The sewing machines buzzed like industrious bees as quilters tried out the latest technology and participated in dozens of available classes. This certainly was different from the stereotypical vision of little old ladies quietly gathered around a quilt frame on a back porch or in a church basement. This was fun!

I knew immediately in the audition process that I would enjoy working with everyone involved, and I was thrilled to be selected to host *American Quilter* and represent AQS. My background as an instructor and facilitator works well in combination with theater and film work. It seems to be a good fit for the role of host: preparing for show segments, working from a script, and meeting and talking with guests about their quilting techniques and projects. This continues to be a wonderful opportunity to work on a quality television production, and I am proud to be part of the American Quilter's Society organization.

Creating a television show is not unlike creating a quilt. Much like a quilt project, the *American Quilter* television series evolved through inspiration, creativity, organization, and determination. The idea for a television series answered the desire to bring the fascinating world of quilting to an

Reviewing the script in the aptly named "Greenroom."

11

Can you hear me now? My friend and professional photographer Skip Atkinson took this photo of the work being performed in a Memphis sound studio.

audience of quilt enthusiasts. To both the well-seasoned quilter and the novice to the craft, the lifestyle format lends a sense of friendly familiarity as, each week, we peek into the lives of quilt artists. We not only get a look at their art and creative efforts, but we also meet their families and friends and get to see how their personal interests inspire their work.

AQS and Context Media, our production group, worked together to piece all the elements of *American Quilter*. From the planning of the stories for location-filmed segments to the organizing and coordinating of studio guests, all the details were meticulously worked out and put into place long distance between AQS in Paducah, Kentucky, and Context Media, in Providence, Rhode Island.

We filmed the pilot episode in early October, and it was a year before all the pieces came together to begin filming the first season at the beautiful home of Marie and Jim Seroskie in New Hampshire.

When I arrived at their home, the film crew had already cleared out Marie's quilt studio and redesigned it as a studio set. AQS had prepared for the event with shipments of dozens of gorgeous quilts to dress the set for thirteen different episodes. Everyone was armed with rehearsal and film schedules, travel itineraries, episode sequences, and scripts. This first day would be a rehearsal to ready for the next day's 7:00 a.m.

call, so after introductions and reunions from the pilot episode, the crew checked the lights, the sound, and the camera positions.

Meredith Schroeder, Helen Squire, and Lynn Lloyd, all from AQS, were on the set every day as technical advisors. They also played host to arriving guests, coordinated wardrobe and quilts, and maintained continuity as we changed sets for the various segments being filmed. This was not always an easy task because the thirteen episodes were filmed out of sequence, according to the availability of our guests.

Under the direction of Curt Worden and his wife, Gloria Balen, our producer, filming was on a tightly choreographed schedule, timed to coordinate with the travel itineraries and rehearsal needs of twenty-six guests. Each day began at 7:00 a.m. with breakfast and make-up. Curt and Gloria assembled a film crew that fit perfectly with our project. They were always professional, personable, and courteous, and they worked diligently to create a quality production. They were as curious about quilting as we were about film production.

How many people worked on the production crew? Well, first of all, the show is filmed simultaneously, with three cameras. The number one, or main camera, focuses primarily on the host and guest, while the second camera films the action from the side. The third camera, known as the "jib," is suspended from a crane, and

it operates in extreme close-up mode to capture the intricate details of quilt work and demonstrations. Our make-up artist and hair stylist matched colors and tones with the wardrobe of the moment and remained vigilant on the set to ensure that we were always our "camera loveliest."

Helen Squire knew which quilts were to be featured and had an eye for coordinating the guests and host with the quilts that dressed the set or were being featured on the show. The sound technician arrived after wardrobe to somehow place our personal microphones so that we could be heard but the apparatus was hidden from the camera's view.

During the sound and light check, Curt would review the script and give directions to those of us on camera. Meanwhile, the lighting director and his crew would move lights about, checking for optimal settings. Around the corner, in the control room behind the sound blankets, Gloria worked with the sound engineer and teleprompter operator to coordinate last-minute script changes and to check the view on the monitors. The three AQS advisors surveyed the set to ensure that the correct quilts were hung and that the sponsors' products were properly displayed. The AD (assistant director) slated the shot to identify the episode, take, and other information for the editing that would take place later in Rhode Island. With that, Curt called for "action" and the cameras were rolling. That was the first half-hour!

As host of the show, I invite the audience into our studio each week to

tion crew, AQS team, guests, and homeowners is what makes the hard work a rewarding experience. Curt and Gloria maintained an

→JEANNA: EACH WEEK, OUR SHOW FEATURES ONE VERY SPECIAL QUILT.

The luxury of working with a teleprompter!

upbeat, amicable working atmosphere, yet there was never any doubt that we were all together for the purpose of creating a professional, first-rate production. In the warm atmosphere of the studio in a real home, we were relaxed and comfortable, and we enjoyed the hours we shared in the New Hampshire autumn.

share "techniques, tips, and lifestyle" with a Savvy Quilter and a guest with his or her Quilt of the Week. Although the introduction and lead-ins are scripted and available on a teleprompter, the conversation around the techniques or quilt displays is not. I learned more in ten days than I could have ever imagined. It was quite a privilege to work with and learn from distinguished guests whom Curt Worden calls "Rock Star Quilters!" It was also great fun to reunite with some of the quilters I had met during the filming of the pilot episode or at the quilt shows I had attended. Each day, I met our guest quilters, who traveled from all over the United States to share their innovative techniques and their magnificent quilts. While we worked together, it was a chance to become acquainted and learn about each other, our backgrounds, interests, and families. It was also the start of several wonderful friendships.

Because filming a show is a collaboration of those in front of and behind the cameras, the interaction of the produc-

Helping me out on a last-minute crisis, our production assistant told me the meaning of a "Doo-Wop." That is a kind name for an honest, but less-than-brilliant mistake. Ask me, and I might tell you a story! —JJ

With the conclusion of the final Quilt of the Week segment, the first season production was a "wrap." Immediately, the crew began to disassemble the set, move a truck-full of equipment outside, and put the household back together again. The reverse transformation took place quickly as cameras, lights, and reels of thick electrical chords were removed and laid alongside stacks of rods and clamps, boxes, blankets, and technical recording apparatus. My husband, Joseph, arrived to watch the last day of shooting and was just in time to help us repack and label several dozen quilts for return shipping to their owners. He joined the three dedicated AQS executives in this fairly intense physical labor, and soon, stacks of boxes were moved to the drive for some unsuspecting FedEx driver.

Over the next three months, Context Media sorted out the footage from the studio shoot, matched it with the location segments, and edited thirteen episodes for the first season. We captured some of the voiceover work in a Memphis sound studio near my home. Voiceover is literally a voice recorded separately from the filming process and subsequently edited "over" specific segments. A good example of this might be a television commercial in which you recognize a well-known celebrity's voice but never see the actor on camera. As you watch the feature stories filmed by our crew at various locations across the country, you listen to my voice narrating and filling in the background information.

The marvels of modern technology made it possible to read a script in a mid-south sound studio, while Gloria and her group of producers were patched in via telephone from the East Coast. They were able to direct the long distance session as easily as if they were outside in the control booth. Once the sound files were completed, the engineer sent them to the editors to perform their technical magic. We were ready for the premiere!

American Quilter debuted on January 29, 2005. Meredith and Bill Schroeder hosted an elegant reception in Paducah. It was held in a beautiful upstairs room overlooking the refurbished downtown and the Ohio River. Curt and Gloria flew in for the festivities, and all of us eagerly awaited the noon hour, when the local television station would air the show for us at the theater downstairs. After a brief introduction, Meredith invited us to share the excitement of our premiere episode. It was so delightful to see the fruits of our labor and to share the pride of our accomplishment.

My relationship with Marie deepened as we talked about the special relationships we each shared with our fathers.

Watching the show at home, I enjoy the satisfaction that comes with seeing the finished production. Each show features the incredible talents of the men and women with whom I was privileged to become acquainted and share my excitement with our viewers. However, it is the stories behind the scenes that make me smile as I remember the fun and camaraderie that comes with working together with AQS staff, guests, and crew. Often, after viewing an episode, I find myself calling or e-mailing one of my new friends to reminisce and share the excitement of seeing the finished, edited, and "ready-for-prime-time" show.

This book provides a glimpse of our experiences behind the scenes while we filmed our first season of "the television show." In the same way that a quilt reflects both the effort and the heart of its creators, our show combines the talents of quiltmakers and film makers to bring the show to life. Come with me "Behind the Seams" and share some of the anecdotes and stories, and meet the wonderful people who are the heart of *American Quilter.*

My sweet and handsome husband, Joseph.

Episode 1

AMERICAN QUILTER

Caryl Bryer Fallert is a shining star in the world of quilting. *American Quilter* traveled to her home and studio outside Chicago for an in-depth look at Caryl's world. Her day begins like that of most people—time to take in the freshness of the morning, a cup of coffee, and a chance to catch up on her e-mail. But that is where the similarities between her world and ours comes to an end.

Internationally recognized for her award-winning art quilts, Caryl has made a profound mark on the world of fiber art. Her organic approach and attention to detail have earned her the reputation for meticulous craftsmanship. Most quilters recognize CORONA II: SOLAR ECLIPSE, and marvel at its beauty and profound use of curve and color. Simply put, Caryl is an artist of the highest caliber.

"For as long as I can remember, I have expressed myself through artwork," she says. "My formal training was primarily in design, drawing, and studio painting." But one day, Caryl wandered into a quilt shop. "It was an epiphany!"

Today, Caryl's work starts with white, one-hundred percent cotton fabric. The fabric is dyed, painted, and printed to create the palette of colors and visual texture used in piecing and appliquéing her images. "The focus of my work engages the spirit and emotions of the viewer, evoking a sense of mystery, excitement, and joy," she says.

Caryl travels the world as a teacher, lecturer, author, designer and savvy businesswoman.

Caryl Bryer Fallert is as warm and artistic as her glorious art quilts. Hers was the first celebrity quilter name in my script. It required several takes for me to sort out what is now a familiar sounding and well-recognized name. —JJ

Episode 1

SAVVY QUILTER

She is funny. She is quirky. She has a passion for precision. And, she is the master of machine work, both appliqué and quilting. She is our Savvy Quilter, award-winning quilter and author, Sue Nickels, of Ann Arbor, Michigan. Sue dropped in to share her extensive knowledge of quilting supplies to help quilters get ready for machine appliquéing and machine quilting.

For machine quilting novices, her advice is to just get started and keep working at it. "The more the techniques are practiced, the easier they become, and don't get discouraged with a technique too early," she says, "because each one takes practice."

She should know, she has been quilting for more than twenty years, and has stacked up a number of awards that give testament to her extraordinary skills. Working with sister, Pat Holly, their quilt THE BEATLES QUILT took Best in Show at the 1998 AQS Quilt Show & Contest., And last year, together they created THE SPACE QUILT that took Best Machine Workmanship at Paducah.

Today, Sue most of all enjoys the experience of quilting. By the way, sharing the experience with a sister can be rewarding, too!

You can see from Sue Nickels' smile that she has a relaxed demeanor that is as warm and charming as her quilts. Sue and her sister, Pat Holly, are so close that, on the set and in real life, they can begin and finish each other's sentences.

—JJ

TIP
Make machine quilting easier by cutting the fingers off rubber gloves and place them on the first two fingers of each hand. The rubber fingers provide a good grip but keep your hands in touch with the fabric.

—*Sue Nickels*

QUILT OF THE WEEK

Have you ever had a passion that consumed you? Well, the Kelly family is passionate about race horses. They train and exercise horses, and Shirley creates beautiful quilts dedicated to their grandeur and heart.

Shirley Kelly of Colden, New York, stopped by the studios with her magnificent quilt TWO MINUTES IN MAY (76" x 40"), celebrating the Kentucky Derby. It beautifully captures a moment of grace as the horses head for the finish line on their first step to winning the Triple Crown of horse racing.

"I love the energy of this quilt," exclaims host Jeanna Juleson. "Shirley has caught the beauty and the power of these thoroughbreds." This quilt has won award after award for its workmanship.

So what is next for Shirley? She is working on a quilt that is a dream come true for a thoroughbred—breaks fast out of the racing gates, gallops around the first turn, and majestically morphs into a beloved carousel horse.

The reverse side of this remarkable quilt shows the winner of the race! Shirley shared with me that the handsome red horse in the middle of the track is her favorite, so she appliquéd it on the back to show him in the winner's circle with a ribbon and a laurel wreath around his neck. —JJ

The true artist, Shirley Kelly dressed in colors to coordinate with her puffins. —JJ

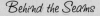

Having read the voiceover script for this segment, I looked forward to seeing the completed piece focusing on these generous quilters. Images of those sweet babies and elderly women wrapped in the warmth of their gifts is a moving tribute to the guild's generosity and love for the community. —JJ

QUILTSCAPES

In the first episode, the *American Quilter* crew took to the road to film the Quilters' Guild of Indianapolis (QGI). The members of this non-profit organization are busy bees (quilting that is), working on their charity quilts. Their work has provided warmth, comfort, and a sense of belonging to thousands of grateful recipients around the Indianapolis area.

The guild started back in 1978 with fewer than twenty members. My, how they have grown. Today, the women and men of the guild number more than three hundred. This group is one of the largest in the country, but nobody can top their need to support their communities with works of charity. For more than a quarter of a century, QGI has "blanketed" the city. Whether it is quilts for the needy, quilts for hospice care, or their amazing quilts for premature babies, they are there with more than three hundred quilts per year.

Every year, for one special night, the members of QGI strut their stuff with a parade of charity quilts, the likes of which you have never seen.

One of their most rewarding works is the preemie quilt program. Tracy Barta has headed this program for some time. She and her merry quilters have made thousands of quilts for the preemie intensive care unit at St. Vincent Hospital in Indianapolis. "Quilts bring a personal touch to an often impersonal place," says one thankful parent. We want to add our thanks, as well, to all the quilters around the world who give of their talents, craft, and hearts every day.

Pieceful Quilter — Norton House in Wilmington, VT

A funny thing happened on the way out of town ...

As is the case with most location filming, some of the funniest and most human events happen off-camera. In the case of this week's shoot with Caryl Bryer Fallert, it happened at the airport as the crew filmed Caryl departing for one of her many teaching engagements.

The day's filming had taken longer than expected, so there was little time left to get Caryl to the airport and capture the footage that director Curt Worden wanted so badly. So, as producer Gloria Bailen stood watch over the crew's van, which was illegally parked in the passenger lane, Curt and cameraman Gilberto Nobrega (far right in photo) ran inside the terminal to capture Caryl's departure. Curt called for an "interesting camera angle." Gilberto dropped down on the terminal floor, filming as much of the activity as possible in the limited time.

Well, it seems a cameraman lying on the floor at an airport, camera rolling, caused a little disturbance. Two burly airport security guards made their way toward the crew, as Caryl hurried to catch her flight. After a little explanation, the crew made a hasty retreat, with camera and film in tow, back to their vehicle and away from the scene. A close brush with the law! Who would have thought that filming a quilt show could get so exciting?

Episode 2

AMERICAN QUILTER

Karen Kay Buckley has inspired quilters from around the world with her beautiful appliqué and can-do attitude. We visit Karen on a beautiful day in Pennsylvania. Karen says that she recently read a wonderful quote from Oprah, "Luck is preparation meeting opportunity. If you hadn't been prepared when the opportunity came along, you wouldn't have been lucky."

That attitude shines bright in Karen and her quilts. It was lucky that she couldn't find a job in teaching after getting her education degree from Lock Haven University in Lock Haven, Pennsylvania. She was working in the insurance industry, filling time, paying the bills, when she enrolled in a local quilting class at the high school. She was hooked! "I sought every quilting class possible to improve my techniques." Then in early 1986, Joe (Karen's husband) was offered an executive position in the Philadelphia area. As luck would have it, part of the incentive to get Karen to agree to the move was the opportunity to open her own quilt shop. The shop also gave her an opportunity to fulfill yet another passion—teach. "I love to quilt. I am also passionate about teaching and enjoy sharing what I have learned with others."

There are two more things you notice about Karen. First is her incredible fabric stash—it's huge and *organized!* Second, she makes perfect circles for her appliqué. Check it out!

SAVVY QUILTER

When Joan Shay is in the room, there is laughter. No two ways about it, Joan is a joy to be with, especially when the set lights are getting hot. But, always one to keep her cool, Joan keeps the show moving with her Appli-bond techniques.

It is a feast of flower gardens on the set, as Joan shows us how to create 3-D roses from cloth. "I have never enjoyed gardening, but I love flowers. Appli-bond allows me to create a weed-free garden that blooms all year long," says Joan.

Everyone got into the act. It was old friends and new friends on the set.

Marie and Jim Seroskie, gracious hosts to the *American Quilter* set, are old friends of Joan's. In fact, Joan and Marie had so much catching up to do that Joan never did show up at the hotel that housed all the guests and crew. Plus, John Flynn was there at the same time, so the laughs just kept coming.

But back to Appli-Bonding. "Two layers of fabric are bonded together, and the design is cut on the line with no seam allowance. If you have bonded the fabric properly, you will not have fraying even when it is washed and dried, and you will be able to curl and shape the pieces," explains Joan. Initially, she concentrated on flowers. It was her kind of gardening—no weeds!

"I have recently discovered the benefit of Appli-bond when creating fish and birds. This technique allows you to construct any appliqué piece with three dimensions. Combine it with traditional appliqué and see how the dimension adds to the realism of the quilt," recommends Joan with a smile!

TIP

To remove paper from iron-on adhesive, score paper with a pin or needle, instead of trying to grab and pull it back from a corner. Just fold the paper back along the score you have made. The paper will crack open, allowing you to remove it.

—*Joan Shay*

QUILTSCAPES

Next stop, the Textile Museum in Washington D.C.—the Blues and Jazz festival is in town and so is the Robert and Helen Cargo collection of quilts. It's improvisational jazz and improvisational quilts—a winning combination.

The crew captures the day's filming with the help of the Textile Museum. Typical of director Curt Worden and producer Gloria Bailen, they needed to delve deeper into the story behind the quilts. So, off to Tuscaloosa, Alabama, to meet with Robert Cargo in person.

Robert and his wife are from Alabama, so it was natural to focus on Alabama quilts, Robert explains. "Everybody was getting central heat, so they had large numbers of quilts they no longer needed." He frequently went to yard sales and never failed to find just exceedingly beautiful quilts. "They came

from the hands of women who were, of necessity, making quilts for family covers," he says.

Yvonne Wells, a retired schoolteacher from Tuscaloosa is one of the award-winning quilters represented in the exhibit. Robert recognized her artistry when he saw some of her first quilts and encouraged her to enter contests and exhibitions. Yvonne believes that people enjoy the simplicity and honesty of her quilts. Her bold, improvisational pieces tell stories based largely on sociopolitical and biblical themes.

Of course, one thing leads to another during spontaneous interviews, and Robert suggested that Curt and Gloria interview the Alabama quilters responsible for part of the exhibition. So the crew seized the opportunity to visit with the quilters in their backyards and on their front porches.

Yvonne Wells

and started the Flynn Quilt Frame Company in Billings, Montana. He sells not only his frames, but also books, templates, and template-making supplies.

QUILT OF THE WEEK

John Flynn, one of our favorite people at *American Quilter*, drops by this week with his FEATHERED SUN quilt. John just brings a new life to the room—tall, burly, and and a quilter to the bone. John brings new life to the room.

John Flynn didn't start out as a quilter. He began his career as an engineer building bridges. One day, while watching his wife Brooke quilt, John's curiosity was sparked. He decided to try his hand at quilting, and then his engineering brain kicked in. There had to be a better way to use a quilting frame. So, he invented one. The rest is—well, you know.

In addition to creating his own breathtaking quilts, John also shares his talents with others as a world-renowned teacher. After several years of quilting, John sold his construction company

Just how many American Quilter crew members and guests does it take to hang a quilt?

Behind the Seams

Episode 3

SAVVY QUILTER

This show's Savvy Quilter is Bethany Reynolds, from Maine, and she is no stranger to the *American Quilter* gang. It is old friends and good times on the set.

Bethany is a quilt teacher, author, and originator of Stack-n-Whack®—you've all heard of Stack-n-Whack. She shows how to make beautiful kaleidoscope quilts that are easy and fun. The method does not involve window templates. In Stack-n-Whack, you prepare (stack) and cut (whack) fabric repeats to make wonderful kaleidoscope, pinwheel, and star designs. As long as the fabric has a good repetitive design, it will work for you.

Each block is different and surprising. Once you have learned this method for one design, you will be able to apply it to many others.

Bethany makes it so easy that everyone is trying it.

Ever-vigilant, with stopwatch, producer Gloria Balen prepares to time Bethany's segment. —JJ

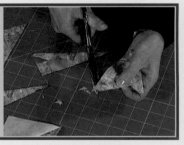

TIP

Trim dog ears (you know, those pesky points) at an angle. This will help reduce the bulk at seam intersections.

—Bethany Reynolds

Amid a very busy schedule, Bethany stopped by American Quilter long enough to share her Stack-n-Whack technique before driving off to other parts of the country to lecture and teach.

—JJ

AMERICAN QUILTER

Gerald E. Roy of Warner, New Hampshire, is dedicated to sharing the world of quilting through teaching, designing, quilting, appraising, and collecting. In this episode, we join him in his New Hampshire home and studio. For inspiration, he likes to take daily walks along the back roads near his New Hampshire home. "I'm constantly looking at things so that I can translate them into my own work," he says. He takes a notebook with him so he can write down descriptions of the world around him, especially of the colors. Then he can bring back a mental picture after he returns to the studio. Originally a land-scape painter, Gerald likes to make quilts that are non-representational in their design. "I want people to bring their own associations to it," he explains. "The intent is to keep the eye moving. I have an image when I start, but I don't try to fix the image before I finish. That keeps the whole process alive for me." Subtle color changes, rather than sharp contrasts, intrigue him most.

As an appraiser, Gerald says that the value of quilts today is pretty much like the value of real estate— location, location, location. But when it comes to quilts, it's condition, condition, condition!

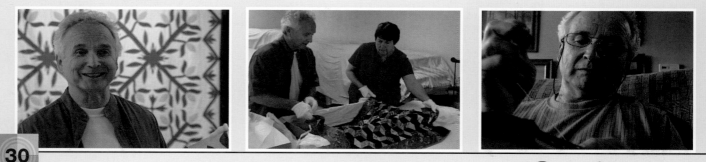

AMERICAN QUILTSCAPE

This week, *American Quilter* focuses the camera on one of its own. All-around quilting expert, designer, teacher, author, and lecturer, Helen Squire has been there, done that (and yes, she has the tee-shirt to prove it).

All kidding aside, Helen's sense of style and passion for quilting makes her perfect for her new role as technical advisor. From wardrobe selection to script review, Helen has her finger in every aspect of the show. It's not all fun and games on the set, though. It's also a lot of elbow grease and a couple of broken fingernails.

With Helen, the crew knows when she has captured the look she is after. "There is the Helen Happy Dance," remarks one of the cameramen. Helen says, "It's all in the design. I don't care if you staple it together, if it's a good design, it will look good. I don't really mean that," she grins. "I'm a perfectionist."

Helen is a star in the world of quilting. She is known world round for her quilting designs. What many people do not know is that Helen Squire is THE Dear Helen!

Endlessly energetic, Helen Squire tends to every detail. We learned she never sits still too long in one place. —JJ

Helen catches the director with a trick question. —JJ

QUILT OF THE WEEK

Linda Carlson from Mexico, Missouri, brought her beautiful AMY'S WEDDING QUILT to the *American Quilter* set this week. An 1870's nine-block quilt made by sixteen-year-old Mary Parks Lawrence, in Russellville, Kentucky, inspired this wonderful four-block quilt. Linda saw this as a great quilt to begin her own family heirloom.

She started it when daughter Amy was only thirteen years old. Linda says that Amy is an outgoing personality, and so she is represented by a cardinal. Linda always pictured that her daughter would marry someone a little bit shy, so she added a bluebird to represent her future husband.

PIECEFUL QUILTER

Today we look in on the bobbin lace demonstration at the AQS Quilt Show in Paducah. It is fascinating to watch. But it has a long and proud history.

Bobbin lace is a technique that resembles both braiding and weaving. A pattern, called pricking, is pinned to a padded surface, the bobbin lace cushion or pillow. Threads are fastened to the prickings with pins. On each thread hangs a bobbin, which also serves as a weight. The threads are then braided in pairs. The structures thus formed are secured with more pins pushed into the cushion. For most techniques you move only four bobbins at a time. You then work through your bobbins in rows (there can be between three and 200+ pairs on a cushion, depending on the pattern), picking up and putting aside pairs as needed. The resulting lace is a fili-gree fabric, in which not only the threads, but the open parts as well make up the design. Some parts look like a net, others like woven fabric and some like braids.

The technique of bobbin lace is very old and was derived from weaving and braiding. Bobbin lace was possibly invented at two locations at the same time—northern Italy and Flanders. The technique then quickly spread throughout Europe and later to North America and Asia.

In Germany it was Barbary Utmann who introduced bobbin lace making during the sixteenth century. This was a welcome source of income for the people of the Erzgebirge Region, because the mines were exhausted, and people didn't have other possibilities to make a living. Very often whole families made bobbin lace—women, men and children. The lace made by women however was considered the most precious, because of their finer fingers. Today lace making is a hobby for most people, but the tradition lives strong in Paducah, Kentucky.

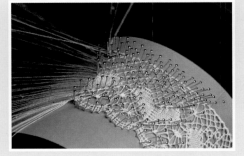

Episode 4

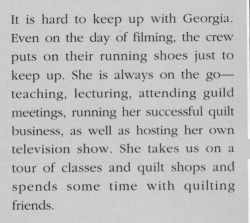

AMERICAN QUILTER

We traveled south to Flat Rock, North Carolina—to the studios of world renowned quilter Georgia Bonesteel. She is unique in the quilting world. Best known for her twenty-seven years of television programs, *Lap Quilting with Georgia Bonesteel*, and her series of books associated with the program, Georgia has made a lasting impact on quilters at home and abroad. Her television series alone has reached millions, in the U.S. and internationally, helping to educate a whole new generation of quilters.

Today, Georgia opens up her personal studio and her quilting life for the *American Quilter* cameras. As one of the founders of quilting on television, Georgia is an integral part of the development of quilting and its accompanying lifestyle.

It is hard to keep up with Georgia. Even on the day of filming, the crew puts on their running shoes just to keep up. She is always on the go—teaching, lecturing, attending guild meetings, running her successful quilt business, as well as hosting her own television show. She takes us on a tour of classes and quilt shops and spends some time with quilting friends.

But when Georgia does take a moment to herself, her beautiful Flat Rock home invites serenity. By the way, did we mention she canoes?

The crew has a great time in North Carolina, even getting on the lake to set up the perfect camera angle of Georgia rowing on the lake. But it's our secret. Don't tell the the director and producer—cameras and water don't mix.

SAVVY QUILTER

Fran Morgan, of Tyler, Texas, is this week's Savvy Quilter. As always, Fran's perky smile and genuine desire to teach make her a perfect co-host for today's show. She shares with the audience her delightful technique for adding chenille embellishments to traditional blocks and her own fanciful quilt designs.

Fran has been sewing since the age of six, and by the time she was a teenager, she had mastered many needle crafts. At the age of eighteen, she went to work for The Needlecraft Shop, Ltd. For this company, she designed more than fifty project books.

In 2000, Fran also became the developing editor for *Sewing Savvy* magazine. After fourteen years with the shop, she decided to work for herself in her home studio. She began experimenting with faux chenille techniques and, after many months, discovered an easy method for replicating the look and feel of old-fashioned chenille.

Fran and her mother, Donna Robertson, had been looking for a way to work together. This amazing mother and daughter team decided that starting a business would only enhance their relationship and, hopefully, their pocket books. They discussed several ideas before Fran began designing in stacked fabric chenille. She introduced Donna to this method, and Donna began experimenting with the process, all the while thinking there had to be an easier way. Discussing the problems and exploring solutions, they created a way to take the work and frustration out of making chenille.

Fran and Donna sought out the expert advise of Robert Scacci, an engineer (and Donna's fiance), to work out the problems of production and their first product, Chenille By The Inch™ was born.

Fabric Café opened its doors in January 2001. Chenille By The Inch was introduced at A Nimble Thimble, a sewing and quilt-

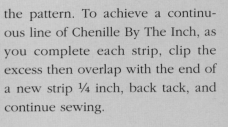

the pattern. To achieve a continuous line of Chenille By The Inch, as you complete each strip, clip the excess then overlap with the end of a new strip ¼ inch, back tack, and continue sewing.

Sandwich the quilt top, batting, and backing. Quilt as desired and bind.

ing shop in Tyler, Texas, on March 16, 2001. It received rave reviews from sewing enthusiasts.

It is a fun adornment. "Watching the chenille strips bloom is a thrill," Fran says, and touching the full, fluffy embellishment is a delight. The possibilities of using this kind of embellishment are endless—garments, hats, bags, toys, and, of course, quilts (contemporary, folk arty, and traditional).

The joy of using the chenille is the easy and distinctive three-dimensional look it gives a project.

HINTS FOR USING CHENILLE BY THE INCH

Use templates for your various appliqué pieces. Trace your pieces onto the back of the Chenille By The Inch.

Once you place your pieces on your block, stabilize blocks with tear-away stabilizer. Use a satin stitch to hold pieces in place.

Remove tear-away backing from Chenille By The Inch. Cut into long strips by centering a straightedge between the stitching lines and cutting with a rotary cutter. Sew Chenille by The Inch strips according to your placement guides on

When it is time to fluff the chenille, use a spray bottle with distilled water to, dampen the sewn chenille strips; using a Chenille Brush, brush vigorously to fluff the strips.

QUILT OF THE WEEK

Sue Gilgen of Madison, Wisconsin, brought her magnificent PEACE MAPLES ON THE TOMOE RIVER (79" x 62") to be displayed on the set of *American Quilter*. American Quilter's Society members are no strangers to Sue Gilgen's quilts. Always a celebration of color and form, Sue's work has graced AQS publications and hung at AQS quilt shows and contests.

Sue created her quilt with no pattern. She likes to work spontaneously and let the fabrics dictate what's going to happen. She has used a lot of free-motion embroidery throughout the piece. "I learned that I can dye, over-dye, paint … whatever is necessary to create the mood or colors I am looking for," she says.

TIP

Sue recommends that you always keep a scrapbook of ideas and a drawing tablet nearby. Then, when ideas come to you, you can get them down on paper while they are still fresh in your mind.

—*Sue Gilgen*

AMERICAN QUILTSCAPE

When you think of Lancaster, Pennsylvania, you probably think of traditional Amish culture, horse-drawn buggies, lush farmland, and quilts hanging from a clothesline. This week's destination is the new Heritage Museum, where Amish quilts are a passion, and the Esprit Collection of Amish Quilts is a prized treasure.

Usually, hip fashion and quilting do not go together. But, in the 1970s, Doug Tomkins founded the Esprit Corporation. He also began collecting these marvelous nineteenth- and twentieth-century Amish quilts that are indigenous to the region. The Lancaster quilts are the brightest and most striking of the quilts from any of the Amish settlements. They are conservative in design but wildly innovative in color.

Initially, the collection was meant to inspire the Esprit designers. The collection hung in the corporate headquarters in San Francisco for many years. The color choices were unusual and beautiful. Designers experimented with the color, texture, and structure demonstrated in the Amish quilts.

But finally, the collection came home to Pennsylvania. The Heritage Center acquired this collection in 2002 and promptly set into motion the development of the Quilt & Textile Museum. The opening of the Lancaster museum on March 31, 2004, marked a new beginning for this historic structure.

The combination of the Esprit Collection with the Heritage Center's own quilt and textile collection results in one of the largest collections of its kind anywhere, presented in context with the stories of south-central Pennsylvanians. The variety and intensity of the collection will leave an indelible imprint on those who view it.

Unlike many quilt museums, this collection hangs within specially lit and climate-controlled glass cases.

Episode 5

Behind the Scenes

SAVVY QUILTER

Karen Combs of Columbia, Tennessee, drops by and the energy level increases tenfold. This dynamo proves the theory that big ideas come in small packages. Karen is the lady with big ideas, creativity and a contagious smile.

Host Jeanna Juleson was in for a few optical illusions in quilting, as Karen describes after-images. "It's kind of like going to an old 3-D movie, except the monster doesn't jump off the screen," says one quilter. "Now it's color that jumps out at you."

Here's a little test: Look intently at any object and then direct your eyes toward a blank surface. Or stare at an area of intense color for a minute or so and then glance away at a white piece of paper or wall. Suddenly, an area of color will appear.

Every color has its own after-image, Karen says. It will be that color's complementary color, which is the one directly across from it on the color wheel. The after-image will be somewhat lighter in value than the original color; for example, the after-image of sky blue is peach. The after-image of clear yellow is a lavender, and so on.

All color tricks aside, this technique works. And, by using Karen's rules, you can make fabulous quilts. And if you see Karen at a quilt show, tell her you learned it all on *American Quilter*.

Finding some professional common ground, the light and camera crews listened attentively to Karen's lesson on color imagery. They share similar techniques when lighting theatrical or film sets, blending color "gels" to achieve the desired light effects. —JJ

TIP

After-images can be used as accent colors in your work. Look for small areas in a design that would be a good placement for the after-image of your primary color. It can fortify the appearance of your dominant color and add to the beauty of your quilt.

— *Karen Combs*

AMERICAN QUILTSCAPE

American Quilter heads out west to Arizona this week. The vast desert sky and mesas are the home to a group of quilters not often seen. Quilt historian Carolyn O'Bagy Davis, from Tucson, introduces *American Quilter* to Hopi quilt-making and visits with Hopi quilter Karen Tootsie and her family. Carolyn describes her first visit to the Hopi villages, perched high on three mesas. "There were quilts everywhere, wrapped around babies, hung on porches, and laid on roofs so people can sit on them to watch the traditional Hopi ceremonies and dances."

Karen tells how her grandmother's quilts inspired her to begin quilting. When she holds the pieces her grandmother made, she remembers what her grandmother meant to her. "It's a family thing," she says.

Since missionaries introduced the craft of quilting to Hopi women one hundred years ago, those simple patchwork bed coverings have evolved into contemporary works of art, incorporating Hopi symbols and designs. Until recently, however, this art form was little known outside the Hopi villages. We are invited inside the homes of Hopi quilters to hear their voices, gain a little insight into their culture and discover how they have adapted this art form to a Hopi tradition uniquely their own. "Our people have always been recognized for the artistry of our pottery, baskets, silver, and kachinas," says Karen. "Now people recognize our quilters, too."

Curt works with Aie for the author book-signing shot. Aie's signature is as lovely as the rest of her art. —JJ

QUILT OF THE WEEK

Now for a change of pace. Aie Rossmann of Calgary, Alberta, Canada, visits the set today. She brought along her beautiful AFFAIRS OF THE HEART (62" x 62") to the set.

An architect by trade, Aie (pronounced like a long A) brings her sense of proportion and Southeast Asian influences to this quilt. In this case, her inspiration came from ancient Burmese temple murals, which provided the heart and scroll designs for her quilt. Every block contains these two designs. Aie says the murals are in muted tones, but she chose to use brilliant colors instead.

Meeting Aie, I was struck by her somewhat quiet and reserved nature, but I soon found that, when you ask her about her children, her demeanor brightens as intensely as her colorful quilts. Not only is Aie an incredibly talented artist, she is also an architect, a career that brought her to the influential Burmese temples. —JJ

AMERICAN QUILTER

"If there is a party going on, Libby Lehman is right in the middle of the festivities—probably teaching everyone how to line dance," says Bonnie Browning. *American Quilter* could not miss this opportunity to visit with Libby Lehman of Houston, Texas, in her studio. This self-confessed "parrot head," zealous reader, and compassionate friend, invites us into her inner sanctuary.

Quilts are everywhere. JOY RIDE, Libby's famous quilt (one of *The Best 100 American Quilts of the 20th Century*) is part of the decor—along with the first quilt she ever made. (Let's all hope we have better quilts to come, too.)

"Making quilts is an utter joy for me," says Libby. At the same time she admits, "Parts of the process can be tedious, but the product is always worth the effort."

She started quilting when her mother, Catherine Anthony, signed them up for a basic class. Libby's unique style, which she calls "threadplay," evolved from years of traditional handwork, which moved to innovation with the machine.

"The making of quilts is woven through my days," says Libby. Her disciplined work style allows her to complete projects. She works on only one quilt at a time, from beginning to end. And "end" for Libby includes photographing the completed quilt and entering notes into her notebook. This process "cuts down on the clutter. Part of my creative process involves an ongoing dialogue with my quilts. Too many voices trying to talk at once would be distracting," she explains.

Libby is a household name among quilters throughout North America and across the seas. She is known for her lectures, classes, quilts, and her award-winning book *Threadplay with Libby Lehman: Mastering Machine Embroidery Technique*. Her innovative creations hang in private, corporate, and museum collections.

Libby has one more source for quilting—her son, acclaimed fly fisherman Les Lehman. They swap threads and gadgets.

PIECEFUL QUILTER
Hobbs Bonded Fibers, Waco, Texas

Batt—literally, the heart of the quilt—gives our quilts structure and dimension. Today, we are off to Hobbs Bonded Fibers to watch batting made and packaged. But, how do you pick the right batting for your project?

Before choosing a batting for your next quilt project, ask yourself the following:

1. How do you want the quilt to feel—fluffy or flat?
2. How do you want it to look—antique or modern?
3. Are you quilting by hand or by machine?
4. Is this quilt to be used as a bed quilt?
   If so, how warm does it need to be?
5. Does the user have any allergies?
6. What color is the quilt? Battings come in a wide range of colors.

The answers to your questions will lead you to the right batting.

Did you know that batting is made from lots of different materials? Polyester battings and polyester blend battings are excellent for a number of projects, including baby quilts. Pure cotton battings are great for an antique feel or the more "organic" among us. Wool battings (usually made from domestic sheep hair) is great for warmth, in that it lets the quilt "breathe" while still providing warmth and comfort on a cold night. Silk batting has gained tremendous popularity in recent years. But did you know there are other types of batting—though rare.

Alpaca batting is now available. Technically, it is a wool batting, but made from the hair of the Alpaca (descendants of camels and cousins to llamas) from the Andes Mountains of South America. In Mongolia, there is a quilt-like blanket made using a soft goat suede as batting. And, of course, there are quilters that make their own batting using old blankets, old quilts, and other fabrics. No matter how you stuff it—commercial batting or something else—the textile sandwich is still a quilt.

Episode 6

LAURA FIS

Sylvia was the he

Behind the

Bonnie continues, "The color of the border plays an important role. A dark border has the effect of lightening and enlarging the quilt center, while a light frame serves to darken and shrink the image." Borders also provide versatility in size and proportion.

Borders should accentuate a quilt. For Bonnie, that means the use of many techniques—curves, pieced and appliquéd borders, and embellishing features, such as bias or cording.

Bonnie is the consummate quilt instructor. Showing her savvy techniques proceeded so smoothly, that a second "take" of her segment was only filmed as a backup or what a director calls a "safety" shot. —JJ

SAVVY QUILTER

In today's show, Bonnie Browning is our Savvy Quilter and she shows us the basics of quilt borders.

Does every quilt need a border? The answer to that question, Bonnie says, is "no." To border or not to border your quilt is one of the design decisions you must make. A border can be added for several reasons:

- to enhance the center of the quilt,
- to define a section or the whole quilt,
- to provide a frame,
- to bring out the colors in the design,
- to stop the design in the center, or
- to enlarge the size of the quilt.

TIP
After sewing pieces together to create your top, measure the top in both directions (horizontally and vertically). Use the measurements to make your border.

—Bonnie Browning

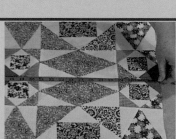

AMERICAN QUILTSCAPE

It's time to put on your roller skates. We are getting the unprecedented tour of behind the scenes in a day with Bonnie K. Browning, executive show director for the annual AQS Quilt Show & Contest. Come along for a madcap ride—and try to keep up.

It's April, dogwoods are in bloom, and there is no better place in the world for quilters to be than at the AQS quilt show in Paducah, Kentucky. Quilters have flocked here from all over North America and from around the world.

The whole city becomes Quilt City USA during the show. And Paducah, Kentucky, opens its doors and hearts to the more than 37,000 attendees that come for the four-day event. There are signs welcoming quilters. There are posters and street flags.

And there are quilts—contest quilts and exhibition quilts—more than 700 on display, plus classes, lectures, award ceremonies, a fashion show, and the best merchant mall around. Bonnie is the mastermind and ringmaster who puts it all together. "Who else gets to plan a party for over thirty-thousand, and they all show up?" jokes Bonnie. After all, for more than ten years, Bonnie has been chief cook and bottle washer.

In reality, Bonnie and her merry Quilt Show band, Cathy Dolson, Jeanie Sullivan, Whitney Jones, and Rita McNabb, have been working on the show for more than a year and half. "By the time the doors open, we've done our work," explains Bonnie. So what is all this running around if not work?

For Bonnie, this is the fun part. The AQS show stretches over half a mile, meandering through hallways and in separate buildings and on different floors. AQS uses other facilities throughout Paducah for special events. "We use every space we can find" to make sure quilters are getting exactly what they have come to expect from AQS—the best!

What's the funniest thing that has ever happened? One year, a quilter fainted in the aisle. As Bonnie and Associate Director Cathy formed a human shield so paramedics could work, a group of quilters spotted a fat quarter sale—the EMTs didn't stand a chance. "They just stepped over all of us!"

Even after ten years as director, a year and half of planning, and four remarkable days of quilt show, you can bet Bonnie is still smiling—sore feet and all!

AMERICAN QUILTER

American Quilter is on the road to the home and studio of Jennifer Chiaverini. Jennifer is your typical quilter—actually, she is not typical at all. In fact, Jennifer is the *New York Times* best-selling author of the Elm Creek Quilt novels. Quilters and non-quilters around the world love the exploits of her marvelous characters.

Meeting Jennifer for the first time last year, I looked forward to seeing the finished segment on our show. I was honored when she asked me to sign a block for one of her upcoming quilts. —JJ

Jennifer Chiaverini's storytelling gift is surpassed only by her knowledge of the art of quilting. Jennifer taught herself to quilt in 1994 and has been stitching, collecting fabric, and accumulating UFOs (unfinished objects) ever since. She wrote *The Quilter's Apprentice*, her first novel, as a gift for the quilters who have blessed her life with their friendship. Her newest book, *Sugar Camp Quilt*, is the sixth book in the Elm Creek series. Readers are drawn to these books. The strong female characters are inspirational, and their quilts are works of art and history. The sense of family and community among quilters is pervasive in her work and in her life.

Jennifer's ability to entwine the craft with the lore makes her a standout novelist. But she is also a quilter's quilter. She has written two additional books that present the patterns for the quilts in her novels. She has also designed a fabric line for Red Rooster Fabrics.

A graduate of the University of Notre Dame and the University of Chicago, Jennifer now lives in Madison, Wisconsin.

QUILT OF THE WEEK

American Quilter takes an unusual turn for Quilt of the Week and heads to the International Quilt Study Group (IQSG) at the University of Nebraska-Lincoln. The IQSG has become an important repository for American quilts. Research focused on quilts illuminates the complex ways gender, class, ethnicity, aesthetics, politics, religion, and technology find expression in the textile arts, quiltmaking traditions, design, and culture.

In this episode, Carolyn Ducey, curator of the IQSG collection, talks about the history of the quilt patterns created by Marie Webster, Anne Orr, and Mary McElwain—three pioneers of the quilting industry. Each developed patterns that were sold to an enthusiastic marketplace. Marie Webster has been credited with having been a leader of the great quilt revival in America during the early part of the twentieth century. She was so admired by other designers that they often "borrowed" her original designs and published them under their own company names, without credit. (The copyright laws did not come into being until 1951.)

Ann Orr similarly created patterns that struck the fancy of quilt-makers in the first half of the twentieth century. She is also known for marketing the first iron-on transfer patterns.

Mary McElwain ran her own quilt shop in Wisconsin, about sixty miles outside of Chicago. Between 1920 and 1940, her shop was considered to be one of the most influential in the country, hosting many quilt dignitaries.

Episode 7

Behind the Sce...

QUILT OF THE WEEK

Diane Gaudynski's quilt THROUGH A GLASS DARKLY: AN AMERICAN MEMORY (80" x 80") is a majestic example of color in motion and exquisite craftsmanship. Diane brings this amazing work to us today.

She makes her home in Pewaukee, Wisconsin, but with her busy schedule as a teacher, author, lecturer, quilt judge, and award-winning quiltmaker, it's difficult to imagine that she has much time to enjoy the Wisconsin landscape, much less the time in her studio to create such beautiful quilts.

The Log Cabin blocks in the quilt contain hand-dyed cottons. The piece is machine quilted with nylon monofilament and silk threads. Many of the gradations of color used in the quilt are based on the color of her cat Fluffy's fur.

The tragedy of September 11, 2002, played a major part in this quilt. As Diane recalls, the initial quilt was full of dark colors. She felt the need to bring "light" to darkened spaces, hence the introduction of the brighter colors.

I met Diane during my first tour of MAQS, where she was teaching one of her highly attended, wait-in-line-for-a-year classes. Filming the quilt of the week with her was a highlight for me, displaying one of her breathtaking pieces and finding out that we both share a deep love for our kitty cats. —JJ

SAVVY QUILTER

If you know Linda M. Poole, you know that the studio is full of laughter any day she drops in to visit. Linda sees the world with a different vision than most of us. Her world is full of color, fanciful images, and inner joy. Her smile is as contagious as her spontaneity.

"I had always been a child with endless questions and energy, so two very smart ladies, my mother and my grandmother, always seemed to teach me and keep me busy with small projects and handwork," recalls Linda. It was the first step of Linda's journey to quiltmaking. Of course, like most of us, Linda didn't realize that it was a journey until she visited a fabric store and saw her first sampler quilt, when she was in her twenties. Now, "my quilting has become my passion for a lifetime," she states.

In this episode, she shows us her new Bended Bias appliqué techniques. It's not stained glass. With Linda's method, bias tape is used to embellish appliquéd blocks. It can also be used in pieced blocks.

She demonstrates using Bended Bias on butterflies—not just any butterflies, but appliqué wonders of Linda's own design. She is passionate about appliqué, and she has developed techniques that make it fun and versatile.

Linda wasn't always that comfortable with appliqué, but she kept at it until she found a technique that worked for her. That's her advice, by the way: "Keep trying."

There really is no one perfect way to do anything."

Linda says, "We are fortunate to be able to choose whether to make our bias tape in a traditional manner or to use the gizmos and gadgets available at our quilt and fabric shops or online. If time does not permit, you can easily buy pre-made fusible tape in a wide variety of colors."

Linda teaches and lectures throughout the country and in Europe. She is also a founding member of the Fairie Goddess Mothers quilting group, (plus she designed the original fairie pattern. She is curating their first exhibition, which is expected to tour at quilt venues across the country.

One of the most hilarious moments happened while filming Linda Poole's Savvy Quilter segment.

Well into her technique and focusing on paper appliqué, Linda calmly and unexpectedly slammed her open palm down on the table. Stunned and somewhat dazed, we all stood silently agape as she matter-of-factly stated that she "must have missed that pesky fly." We were able to continue after our laughter subsided and our hearts began beating again at a regular interval.

TIP

Before bias tape can be made, the fabric needs to be washed and ironed. Then cut a square of fabric in any convenient size. Fold it in half diagonally and iron the crease. Use a rotary cutter and ruler to cut along the crease. Then, from both pieces, cut strips the desired width as measured from the diagonal cut.

—Linda Poole

AMERICAN QUILTER

For a different look at what constitutes a quilter and a quilt, we are off to the Tampa, Florida, studio of Fraser Smith. When you enter Fraser's studio, you are struck by the beautiful and intricate patterns of his quilts—that and the fact that his quilts give a whole new meaning to the expression "knock on wood." That's right. Fraser carves his quilts out of blocks of basswood.

He wanted to explore something completely different in his sculpting and found that quilts provided a challenging subject. Quilters love his work as much as he loves theirs.

Fraser creates the feel of a quilt by carefully sculpting the wood. Then, using his artist's eye, he colors the pattern in the wood with stains.

AMERICAN QUILTSCAPE

The Museum of the American Quilter's Society (MAQS) is a diamond by the river in Paducah, Kentucky. Founded in 1991 by Bill and Meredith Schroeder, it is the only quilt museum dedicated to contemporary quilts. Today, more than 60,000 visitors come through the doors of MAQS to see the constantly rotating collection of quits created by the top artists of today.

From the start, Bill and Meredith envisioned a museum that would display quilts in such a way that they could be viewed as important works of art. At the same time, the pieces would be carefully preserved for future generations.

For Bill, it's an emotional experience to walk through the galleries and see what quiltmakers have accomplished. For those who may think that quiltmaking is not an art form, they need to visit the Museum of the American Quilter's Society!

Episode 8

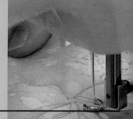

SAVVY QUILTER

Everyone gets into the act of quilting, with Sally Terry of Paducah, Kentucky, as our Savvy Quilter.

Sally describes her concept of the five quilting shapes. They are the arc (or C-curve), the S-curve, the straight line, the loop, and the hook. You will find these shapes in almost every quilting pattern, whether it is a stencil, a printed pattern, or a pantograph for longarm machine quilting. Combined, they form thousands of patterns.

She tells us that, as you become more proficient by practicing the five shapes, you will gain the freedom to create and execute any quilting motif.

TIP

When working with very busy fabric, try using a variegated thread. It will blend with all of the colors in the fabric.

—*Sally Terry*

PIECEFUL QUILTER

The show always ends with the Pieceful Quilter. And today, we watch the masterful hand quilting of Virginia "Rusty" Hedrick. She is in complete control of the needle—with precise stitches, she quilts in any direction. Rusty is artistry in motion.

QUILT OF THE WEEK

Gail Garber was all smiles on the set of *American Quilter*, after her long trip from Albuquerque, New Mexico. Host Jeanna Juleson marvels at the beauty of Gail's quilt COSMIC PARADE. Gail describes the design as a parade of colorful stars, while equally colorful geese wander through the parade. The yellow, she says, keeps the eye moving through the quilt.

She created her quilt by combining traditional Flying Geese and star patterns. The 50" x 67" quilt is machine pieced and machine quilted. The fabrics were hand-dyed by Mickey Lawler.

Helen Squire acted as wardrobe mistress: Didn't she color-coordinate us well for this cosmic Quilt of the Week?. –JJ

We found out one more fascinating thing about Gail—she is the executive director of Hawks Aloft, a non-profit organization that works to conserve birds of prey and other wildlife through research and educational programs. "Hawks Aloft conducts a variety of avian research and survey projects in New Mexico. Each is designed to increase our knowledge of raptors, passerines, and the habitats they occupy," says Gail.

No wonder she is attracted to the Flying Geese pattern. Maybe we need a new pattern named for her beloved hawks? Thank you, Gail, for bringing your beautiful quilt and for all your work to save the raptors.

AMERICAN QUILTSCAPE

This week, *American Quilter* is headed to St. Charles, Missouri, for a one-of-a-kind event—Quilts on Main.

It is a truly unique art show, and it is held every fall. Hundreds of colorful quilts are displayed on the facades of vintage buildings that line fourteen blocks on historic Main Street. The amazing diversity of patterns and color is impressive. Set amidst the quilt displays, there are quilt guild demonstrations and quilt raffles, and all of it is open and free to the public.

The quilt show is totally funded by advertisers and sponsors, and it is staffed by volunteers. Many shop owners contribute to the festivities by placing quilts in their windows and along ledges and balconies, anywhere they can

think of. The rest of the quilts are hung by the quilt show volunteers, who have to get up before daybreak to get everything done before the show opens. The display of such beautiful art is a sight to behold, and it's wonderful to see so many people on Main Street, appreciating the beauty and craftsmanship of these designs.

Whether you are an art lover or a quiltmaker, Quilts on Main is a thrilling experience not to be missed, but there is more. The St. Charles Civil War Reenactment and All-American Weekend coincides with the festivities of Quilts on Main. The combination of the two events allows visitors the rare opportunity to understand the history and necessity of making quilts, while enjoying the beautiful contemporary pieces. Without a doubt, it's a grand weekend to be in St. Charles.

AMERICAN QUILTER

What could be more fun than a bus load of your favorite quilting friends and a road trip to the AQS Quilt Show & Contest in Paducah, Kentucky? Two bus loads, that's what!

We join two groups of Wisconsin quilters who have made this April trip for years. Janice Armagost and Sharon Doyle are the masterminds behind this great adventure. The two are sisters, close friends, quilters—and arch rivals as soon as the buses pull out of Madison, Wisconsin.

Each sister leads one bus load of quilters, who have one thing on their minds—spend, spend, spend. The bus load that spends the most money over the four days at the show wins!

First stop, Hancock's—let the games begin! Next, the quilt show! After three days, the spending frenzy winds down, and both teams gather for a spirited show-and-tell. "We're making up our husband lies," says one contestant.

As the buses are loaded for the return home, one bus driver laughingly complains, "These bags are a lot heavier now than when they came." The group leaders gather up the receipts. The result, bus one, $35,803.74; bus two, $48,418.85. Good Friends, Priceless. But no one really lost. They still have all their goodies, and next year …

.

Episode 9

QUILT OF THE WEEK

Today, Nancy S. Brown of Oakland, California, shares with us her quilt THE NIEBUR SISTERS. This 52" x 46" hand appliquéd and hand quilted work represents a personal voyage for Nancy. She is known for her marvelous quilted animals, but this time, she took a family heirloom photograph, created an appliqué pattern from it, incorporated a traditional block pattern in each corner, and used period fabrics to create this wonderful tribute to four endearing sisters, among whom is Nancy's great-grandmother.

Nancy told us that many people think the most difficult part of quilting the Niebur Sisters was piecing together the faces. However, she suffered the most angst trying to replicate the intricate details of the fancy shoes. —JJ

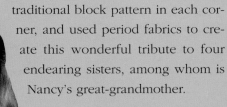

Nancy is a lot of fun on the set, and she really bonded with the crew—using production manager Roger Yergeau as a "table" (see photo at right). The crew didn't mind, especially with Nancy's mad sense of humor driving them on. By the way, did you know that Nancy Brown is a cartoonist?

Nancy and the crew.

Everyone enjoyed hearing Nancy talk about her great-grandparents, the subject of our "Quilt of the Week." Suddenly, the cartoonist side of our somewhat quiet guest emerged; as you can see, she had everyone on our crew laughing and was quickly surrounded for a memorable shot.

using fabric or fiber, he may select elements such as tin, microfilm, Mylar, and acetate.

"What distinguishes me from other artists working in fiber is my choice to mainly explore and recycle twentieth-century industrial materials which have been primarily designed as tapes or films. Incorporating them into woven or interlaced webs provides for me permutations for my design concepts, which are personalized into a visual vocabulary of the sky, water, landscape; and more recently, issues

related to international and domestic politics, terrorism, the total nuclear threat, the cosmic realms, and personal spiritual beliefs," states Arturo.

For serenity, he has created a meditation garden that includes art.

AMERICAN QUILTER

Today, we offer you a feast for the senses. It is what you see, hear, and feel that will be remembered, not just the words.

American Quilter goes to Lexington to visit the home and studio of Arturo Alonzo Sandoval. One of Kentucky's most original and influential fiber artists and professor of art at the University of Kentucky, Arturo has earned the respect of his students along with an international reputation. His pieces grace collections in the Museum of Modern Art in New York City and the Indianapolis Museum of Art, and in galleries and private collections throughout the world.

Arturo started his artistic journey as a weaver, then later discovered that several men in his family had also been weavers. His distinction is his ability to recycle industrial materials and incorporate them into expressive interpretations. For his creations, instead of

Marie Seroskie

SAVVY QUILTER

Our heirlooms, those fabric treasures from family and friends, are precious, and Bobbie A. Aug is here to show us how to preserve them. Bobbie is a quilt teacher, lecturer, collector, book author, authority on antique quilts and textiles, as well as a quilt appraiser and appraising instructor.

Here are Bobbie's recommendations for protecting quilts and other textile heirlooms:

One reason to preserve textiles is to pass on examples of quiltmaking to future generations. To accomplish this, it is necessary to be aware that textiles are sensitive to light, chemicals, dust, dirt, oils, smoke, stains, perfumes, and excessive washing, and they will absorb odors and moisture. Quilts or quilted textiles should be aired or vacuumed before storing. Use a small, low-suction hand vacuum with a nylon screen over the quilt to protect it from harmful pulling. When airing a quilt, be sure it is lying flat, protected from soil, back and front, and not in direct sunlight. The ideal storage is a flat surface, properly lined with acid-free material and large enough for each quilt to have its own space.

Strive for a constant environment. Heat, moisture, and extreme cold cause fabric deterioration. The herb Artemisia (southern wood variety) is a natural pesticide. Hang it in the storage area in a small bag. Do not allow the bag to touch the stored quilts or quilted textiles.

Bobbie stresses how important it is to have your quilts and textiles appraised by a certified appraiser. A written appraisal allows the item to be properly insured in case of loss or damage, and inventoried for estate planning. It also provides an understanding of its historical significance.

TIP

Use rolled acid-free tissue in the folds. Or use a noodle float (for swimming pools) wrapped in muslin for storing and shipping. The tube helps protect quilts with thread painting, fused appliqué layers, or heavy machine quilting.

—Bobbie Aug

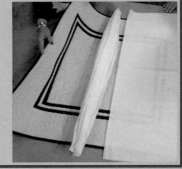

Helen Squire

AMERICAN QUILTSCAPE

It's Music City USA meets Quilt City USA in Nashville, Tennessee, that is! The quilters are in town, and they are having a ball. It's fun, friends, and quilts all around. It's the AQS Quilt Exposition, held every year in August at the famed Gaylord Opryland Hotel and Resort.™

Bonnie Browning, executive show director for AQS, explains that the Quilt Exposition at Nashville is a completely different kind of show from the famed AQS Quilt Show & Contest in Paducah. "Just the ambiance of the Gaylord Opryland facility is different, plus the quilt contests have a completely different theme. It's another great AQS show, but with a twist."

One twist is the Ultimate Guild Challenge with $5,000 in prizes. In this contest, quilt guilds issue a challenge to their members. The guild then selects the top eight challenge quilts to enter the contest. The resulting exhibit is marked by originality and full of surprises—a very popular exhibit in Nashville.

"It was never our intention to replicate the Paducah AQS

Quilt Show and Contest," says Meredith Schroeder, president of American Quilter's Society. "This show has its own life, its own flair." Part of it is the facilities. The aisles are wider and all the exhibitions and merchant mall are housed in one facility. "That creates part of the atmosphere," says Meredith. "Plus, the quilters can just stay here at the resort, enjoying the the quilt show, the gardens, a choice of restaurants, and entertainment."

But the show is still all AQS. The AQS staff are here to make sure our members and friends have a good time.

Even Bill Schroeder, co-founder of the American Quilter's Society, is having a good time as he plays "guard" at the show entrance.

This year, the Fairie Goddess Mothers are here to celebrate and show off their Fairie Exhibit. And the "Janiacs" come by in large numbers for a reunion. Plus the AQS School of Quiltmaking has everybody working on new techniques and perfecting their craftsmanship.

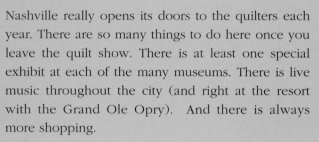

Nashville really opens its doors to the quilters each year. There are so many things to do here once you leave the quilt show. There is at least one special exhibit at each of the many museums. There is live music throughout the city (and right at the resort with the Grand Ole Opry). And there is always more shopping.

It seems appropriate that AQS started a quilt show here in 2000. After all, it was just down the road in Bell Buckle, Tennessee, in 1983 that launched the American Quilter's Society. Now entering our third decade, we are still dedicated to Today's Quilters. So come celebrate quilting in Music City USA—Nashville!

PIECEFUL QUILTER

Let's join the Mennonite Relief Committee of Lancaster County, Pennsylvania, as they create a quilt of beauty and style in the tradition of Amish quilts. The quilt was later auctioned for charity. The craftsmanship of hand quilting is evidenced in the graceful rocking of the needle by this skilled quilter.

Episode 10

Behind the Seams

SAVVY QUILTER

Who can resist that smile? Plus she makes and designs fabulous quilts. The cast and crew of *American Quilter* welcome author, teacher, lecturer, and award-winning quilter Suzanne Marshall of Clayton, Missouri.

Suzanne's specialty is take-away appliqué. She has won top quilt contests around the world, and a quilt of hers was chosen as one of the Twentieth Century's 100 Best American Quilts. She was also selected to be included in the 30 Distinguished Quilt Artists of the World Exhibit in Tokyo, in 2003.

About her technique, she says, "I love using notebook paper for templates because it is inexpensive, and it has lines on it. I use the lines to match the grain lines on the appliqué piece with the grain lines on the background fabric. Not only do I like the look of matched grain lines, it solves warping and rippling problems on a long piece to be appliquéd."

the order they will be appliquéd, cut the first pattern piece and use it as a template for cutting the fabric piece. Appliqué it down and proceed to the next piece. "My first appliqué project was a mess," she says. Now her quilts are masterpieces.

Her basic technique gave Suzanne a way of handling complicated patterns one piece at a time. On the simplest of levels, you trace your pattern onto notebook paper. Then, in

TIP

For hand appliqué, turn under only enough fabric to make one stitch. After all, you only have to make one stitch at a time.
—*Suzanne Marshall*

AMERICAN QUILTER

Patricia B. Campbell is originally from Michigan, but she is now a Texas girl, making her home in Richardson, north of Dallas. The *American Quilter* heads to the Lone Star state to visit with Pat in her studio.

Pat tells us how she got started in quilting: "I took my very first class in 1984," says Pat. "I always wanted to make a Victorian crazy quilt. I thought it would be a wonderful thing to own one. I walked into a quilt shop in the Tampa Bay area of Florida and asked about it. The owner said, 'Honey, you don't make those. You buy those,' " Pat recalls.

"I asked her, 'Now what do I do?' She said, 'Go to the back of the room. They're teaching a quilting class.' Well, I saw what they were doing. It was handwork, and I had always liked doing handwork. So I took that first class, and within a year, I was teaching at her shop."

Pat turned her passion for quilting into a career. She is an award-winning appliqué artist, as well as an exciting speaker and inspiring teacher. She fell in love with the seventeenth- and eighteenth-century Jacobean designs. The stitches in Jacobean embroidery do not differ from other forms of needlework, but the thread and design do differ. An air of fantasy and romance permeates the compositions, which are usually floral or arboreal with deeply

notched leaves, undulating vines, intertwined branches and stems, coiling tendrils, and imaginative flowers. It was this movement of form and color that first attracted Pat's attention to the embroidery.

A new quilt-art form was created when Pat, retaining the spirit of the antique pieces, began transforming the old Jacobean embroidery designs into new Jacobean appliqué designs.

Her designs are based on classic botanical shapes, which have been simplified for appliqué. Focused on fantasy rather than realism, they are charming and fun to stitch.

It is no surprise that Pat found the Jacobean style wonderful. After all, she is an avid flower gardener, with a special love of the English-style garden. More recently, though, she has been adapting her flowers to reflect a slightly more modern look.

Despite her active schedule, Pat is still a member of her original quilt guild. Meeting regularly to go over projects and encourage each other's work, this is a guild that has bonded on much deeper levels. As one member says, "We've been through everything together—that's just the way it is. We are sisters."

QUILT OF THE WEEK

Famous for his crisp white shirts and his sporty bow ties, Bill Lyle, along with wife Jean, are recognized as antique quilt authorities throughout the country. You will likely see them at major quilt shows.

Hailing from Quincy, Illinois, Bill and Jean Lyle have been on the forefront of collecting, authenticating, and insuring antique quilts. Before joining Jean on the road, Bill ran his own independent insurance company. Knowing the value of quilts first hand, Bill pioneered insurance programs to protect these valuable, prized possessions.

For the Quilt of the Week, he brought two beautiful examples of high-quality and well-preserved quilts dating from the 1800s: a Mariner's Compass and a two-sided Log Cabin.

Bill explains some of the things he looks for in antique quilts. He says that this Mariner's Compass is a unique example of the use of color and subject matter, and the oak leaves balance the overall design. He says that an antique quilt from this time and in this condition would easily bring as much $5,000.

QUILTSCAPES

There is nothing like a state fair—the smell of corn dogs and popcorn, the sounds of carnival rides, and the laughter of people out enjoying a fall day. We are off to Kansas, specifically Hutchinson, for the Kansas State Fair.

Kansas, like so many other states, celebrates its proud tradition of agriculture and home economics. This year, more than 337,489 people visited the Kansas State Fair during its September run.

The fair has all the standard attractions—champion livestock, great country-western entertainment, and a rodeo. And they have some of the toughest competition around for the arts and crafts, passed down from generation to generation, including our all-time favorite—quilts!

Over in the Domestic Arts Building, there's a quilting bee going on. Quilters, and soon-to-be quilters, can take a moment, sit down, thread a needle, and join in. The quilting bee, gives everyone a chance to take part in this time-honored tradition. "We want to have the hands-on experience for our attendees," says one of the quilt volunteers. After the fair, these quilts will be donated.

There are competition quilts hung throughout the building, showing off some of the finest craftsmanship around. Competition is intense this year. Hundreds of quilts were entered and judged on design and craftsmanship. Congratulations to this year's winning exhibitors. It takes a lot of hard work, dedication, time, and effort to be in the winning circle.

The top quilts are honored with special recognition. Kansas Governor Kathleen Sebelius stops by to admire the quilts and give out awards.

Episode 11

SAVVY QUILTER

Meredith Schroeder, executive producer for *American Quilter*, invited Debbie Bowles, from Burnsville, Minnesota, to the set as co-host and Savvy Quilter, knowing that it was more than just her "curvy" quilts that set her apart. It's her attitude. "I don't do competitive quilting," says Debbie. "I am totally in awe of those of you who do."

For Debbie, it is the process of creating that keeps her quilting and designing. "Sewing soothes the soul no matter what else is happening in my life," she explains. Of course, Debbie just loves to develop easy ways for all of us to make fantastic quilts, by using interesting approaches to some of our old favorites. "That's what I'm here to teach today," says Debbie.

Making curves from straight pieces adds interest and flair—and it is easy to do. Debbie starts by cutting same-sized squares from several fat quarters. With two different squares layered, both face up, she uses her rotary cutter to cut the squares into four strips of approximately equal width, but she uses shallow, free-form S curves instead of straight lines for her cuts. Her cuts are free-form, but the process works as well if you would prefer to use a template.

Because both squares are cut exactly the same way, the curvy strips in one block can be substituted with those from the other block. The two blocks are then reassembled by alternating strips

Tall, elegant Debbie Bowles' unique cutting technique adds a curvy artistic element, simple enough for beginners. —JJ

TIP
For curves, use the back of your cutting mat. You do not need the lines on the front, and the back is wonderfully smooth, with no gouges catch the cutter.
—*Debbie Bowles*

of different colors. Debbie does not use pins to sew the strips together in their new configuration.

You can use this method of making curved pieces in other traditional blocks—how about a curvy Log Cabin?

AMERICAN QUILTER

If you travel to Bucyrus, Ohio, you are likely to hear about that "quilt lady." And you just might see her with her husband, Dick, bicycling around town or on a country road. Well, that quilt lady is Anita Shackelford, internationally known quiltmaker, author, teacher, and lecturer. Today, *American Quilter* takes you into Anita's world.

Anita is a businesswoman, and likes it that way. She prides herself on the ability to prioritize her work, manage time, and balance several schedules at once. She has a lot to balance these days: running a web business, teaching, lecturing, judging (she's certified by NQA), designing, writing, finding time to make new quilts, and very important to Anita—family time. For Anita, it's all about following your heart. "Make the quilts you want to make," she says. "I try to keep a good balance between 'users' and 'keepers.' Many of my quilts are elaborate, and those are not meant for everyday use."

Anita is known for her ability to combine nineteenth-century dimensional appliqué techniques and fine hand quilting with her original designs. "I love everything about mid-nineteenth century quilts, and I continue to be inspired by them," she says. Anita uses many quilts that she has collected over the years for inspiration. As a beginning quiltmaker in 1967, she wanted to recreate some of the designs she saw in the older quilts but also wanted to add her own ideas and color sensibilities. It is this approach that sets Anita's work apart. "In the early 1980s, I designed two family album quilts, made with original designs and

numerous awards. Of course, people began asking how she made them, so she began teaching in 1980. "I guess you could say that the career found me," she laughs. Anita now travels extensively for shops, guilds, and conferences to teach and demonstrate her techniques.

Known for her exquisite hand quilting, Anita has exhibited her quilts in shows across the United States and in Australia. She has won many awards, including twelve best of shows and many workmanship awards. Two of her quilts have received the Mary Krickbaum Award for best hand quilting at National Quilting Association shows.

Never satisfied with just doing the same thing, Anita has now gone digital. With her daughter, Jennifer Shackelford-Perdue, Anita is embracing state-of-the-art, hands-free quilting on a longarm quilting machine.

incorporating a number of dimensional techniques inspired by the nineteenth-century quilts," she explains. Anita put these quilts in a competition, and they won Anita still loves handwork but now likes to combine the two, using the machine where the quilting doesn't show and hand quilting where it does.

were first seen together at the exhibit, entitled *Double Vision—Companions and Choices: An Exhibition of Quilts and Paintings*, curated by Rod.

The sisters have been quilting together and winning awards for some time. In 1998, Pat and Sue created THE BEATLES QUILT, which won Best in Show at the 1998 American Quilter's Society Quilt Show & Contest. Then again in 2004, the sisters took home the machine workmanship award, at the twentieth anniversary AQS show, for their piece named THE SPACE QUILT. Today, both quilts proudly hang in the Museum of the American Quilter's Society.

Although they live many miles apart in different cities, Sue and Holly somehow manage to work and complete their quilting projects together.

—JJ

QUILT OF THE WEEK

Pat Holly and Sue Nickels share more than award-winning quilting. They are sisters and friends. Today, they stop by the studio with their exquisite quilt NEW YORK STATE OF MIND (69" x 69"). This piece represents yet another collaboration by the sisters.

Initially, painter Rod Buffington asked the sisters to create a quilt as part of an invitational exhibit, featuring quilts by artists from around the United States. Each quiltmaker chose a quilt pattern and sent it, accompanied by fabric swatches, to Rod. Rod then used the colors from the swatches and the quilt pattern to create a painting.

The quilt artist and the painter did not get to see each other's work beforehand. The quilts and the paintings

Behind the Seams

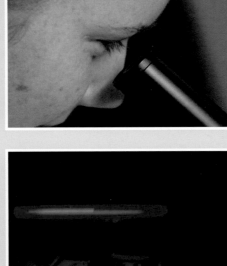

While the researchers are referred to as "quilt detectives," you may notice that the production music adds an element of fun to this segment with its playfully mysterious tone. —JJ

QUILTSCAPES

American Quilter is headed to the Great Plains where, in 1997, Ardis and Robert James donated more than nine hundred quilts to the University of Nebraska-Lincoln. The university responded by establishing the International Quilt Study Center (IQSC) and created a graduate program in textile history with an emphasis on quilts.

This one-of-a-kind program strives to study the quiltmakers of the past and present. IQSC does this by investigating the quilts and the materials used to create them. Approximately seventeen hundred quilts are archived at the center. They are cataloged, stored in acid-free containers, and kept in a climate-controlled environment.

The IQSC is a leader in the burgeoning field of quilt studies. The research work performed within these walls helps provide the framework that illuminates the ways that gender, class, ethnicity, aesthetics, politics, religion, and technology find expression in textile arts.

Quilts are particularly important records of human progress and achievement. As part of a master's degree in textile history, students in the Artifacts and Analysis class learn how to become detectives, using an approach that includes research, examination, and cultural analysis. Daily, students and faculty hunt for the keys that unlock our past, capturing those memories forever.

Episode 12

Pat Yamin, shown here with Lynn Lloyd of AQS and Jeanna, brought her trademark "Come Quilt With Me" pins for both cast and crew. —JJ

SAVVY QUILTER

She's outgoing, outspoken, and always on the move. Pat Yamin, originally from the Midwest (though you would never know it from her accent) came from her home in Brooklyn, New York, to be with us today.

This former high school guidance and vocational counselor knows a little something about prioritizing your life and time. When Pat went to New York for her master's degree, she discovered that quilting supplies were hard to come by and that classes were even harder to find. She started teaching a few classes in the evenings, after work. Pat's classes become popular, and in no time, she was teaching four nights a week in Manhattan, conducting workshops in her home studio on the weekends, and working full-time in counselling. It was time to make a leap to quilting full-time. She started Come Quilt With Me in 1981. The rest, as they say, is history.

This amazing dynamo is always on the go. Pat is the creator of cutting-edge tools for quilters, including her Back-to-Basics patchwork templates and revolving turntable. Pat believes anyone can make fast and accurate quilt blocks. "The most common shapes in the old patterns are the square, half-square triangle, and quarter-square triangle," explains Pat. Blocks from six to twelve inches are standard. From these basic shapes, you can make thousands of blocks.

"I raise all of my cutting tables to forty-two inches," Pat says. "This is a good height for me. It makes cutting easier and faster. I also recommend using the Brooklyn Revolver™ rotating cutting mat. With it, you can cut along each side of the square, rotating the cutting mat while still holding down the template. You can cut, rotate, and cut again, and never move the template or the fabric, so you are guaranteed accurate cutting, which is essential.

After cutting one square, you can then move the template along the fabric strip to cut another square, the same as the first."

QUILT OF THE WEEK

Martha Nordstrom of San Diego has brought MINIATURE ROSE GARDEN FOR JESSIE as our Quilt of the Week. This magnificent gem is a tribute to miniature-quilt artist Jessie Harrison. This tiny garden is a true feast for the eyes. The delicate use of color and fabric is a testament to the adage that great things come in small packages.

Miniature quilts are a special craft form all unto themselves. With their intricate designs and amazing workmanship, they rival their big sisters in beauty. Martha's quilt for Jessie Harrison contains tiny pieces that create a bountiful garden of yellows and pinks. All hand worked, the quilting is as intricate as the appliqué.

Jessie Harrison, another San Diego resident, was a giant in the world of miniature quilts. She believed that her background as a computer professional in the aerospace industry had prepared her for designing these small wonders.

Since 1994, Jessie has won fourteen awards in our annual Miniatures from the Heart Contests. She has also won numerous awards in the miniature quilt category at prominent shows across the country. With her untimely death last January, the entire quilting world suffered a great loss. She left a legacy for all of us and for future generations to enjoy. Admirers, like Martha, will keep Jessie's traditions alive.

We are sure that Jessie would have loved Martha's amazing tribute to her skills.

The intricacy of this work reveals the tiniest details of bird nests and buzzing bumblebees. —JJ

TIP

At the end of a quilting project, we all have leftover fabric pieces. Rotary cut them into two-and-a-half-inch squares and put them in a box. The next time you need a quick and easy gift, use these precut squares. With them, simple block quilts will be fast and easy, and a greatly appreciated by the receiver.

—Pat Yamin

QUILTSCAPES

American Quilter travels to the studio of Rebecca Barker, outside Cincinnati, Ohio, for creative artistry that makes Rebecca's work a favorite among quilters around the world.

Her "quilts" capture many beautiful land-scapes, including farm scenes, lakes, grand prairies, and mountain tops. They evoke the feeling of storms at sea, brilliant sunshiny days, and the exhilaration of flying high above the earth. The quilts are created from traditional appliqué patterns and pieced blocks.

She lovingly pulls her patterns from quilt history books and her inspirations from various quilt shows she attends each year. But there is no fabric or batting or backing in these quilts. Rebecca creates her masterpieces with masonite board and acrylic paint.

Growing up on her family's Oxford, Ohio, dairy farm, where quilting was a pastime for the Barker women, Rebecca developed a deep appreciation for quilts and the country landscape. It was a natural progression to incorporate quilt imagery into her landscape paintings. Rebecca began this wonderful series of Quiltscape paintings in 1994. She has exhibited at national quilt shows and fine art shows. Her quilts can also be seen on her web page. From her works, Rebecca has developed a line of note cards, limited edition prints, and many other gift items. There are quilter's jigsaw puzzles, as well.

Rebecca is a formally trained fine artist, who received her undergraduate degree from Ohio University. She went on to study at Miami University's graduate painting school. Initially, Rebecca was nervous about her ability to make a living with her painting. Of course, today she has overcome that fear and has been successful at her chosen field.

Rebecca lives on the west side of Cincinnati in a quaint, old farmhouse, which also serves as her studio. Once she has decided on a pattern from her research, she proceeds with the painting. "I do not make up the patterns. I love the designs of old quilts," she remarks. She creates her own color combinations and makes decisions about materials.

She says, "My work is meant to honor the beauty of the old-time quilts and their makers."

Rebecca Barker's paintings are truly loved and appreciated by all who view them.

AMERICAN QUILTER

If one person fits the famed title *I Dream of Africa,* it would be Hollis Chatelain. Not only does she dream of her beloved friends and the landscape of West Africa, she captures it in her art. It is in her quilts, that her love and deep appreciation for people shine through.

These days, Hollis is trying to show more respect for her dreams—often the place where the images and underlying messages for her art quilts originate.

This beautiful woman has led an extraordinary life. Hollis Chatelain was born and raised in Pennsylvania, but took up the challenge of the Peace Corps, spending twelve years in West Africa. It was there that her career as a textile artist was born. At the end of 1996, she moved back to the United States, with her husband and three children. She now makes her home in North Carolina.

Though she was educated in design and photography, it was the rich and vibrant African fabrics that moved her artist's eye toward fabric. Her distinctive use of colors and imagery and her dye-painted scenes of multi-cultural life have brought Hollis international recognition.

Hollis says, "Much of my work is influenced by my personal experiences. I make imagery that evokes an emotional response and creates a mood or atmosphere. My dreams also provide me with an infinite supply of inspiration and reinforce my views and feelings. When I am at peace, I dream images, and color flows. When my life is chaotic, I dream people and events. My dreams are lucid and always in color."

It is the people and their lives that provide a foundation for her work. "The twelve years I lived in Africa have deeply influenced me. Six months after moving back to the United States, my longing for Africa was so great that I started to paint African images in order to put me back into the life I loved so much. I feel Americans should know more about the joy, harmony, and pride of the African people, rather than only hearing about the suffering and turmoil so commonly depicted in the media. I would like viewers to see my African imagery as a tribute to a people I truly admire and respect."

Hollis is not limited to African subject matter. "Since 2000, much of my work has reflected my feelings on world-wide issues. Whether these concerns be social or environmental, they have overwhelmed my dreams and manifested themselves in my art."

Episode 13

Behind the Seams

QUILTSCAPES

In this episode, quilt historian Rachel Pellman talks to Amish women from Lancaster County, Pennsylvania. This county has the oldest Amish settlement in the United States, with more than sixteen thousand people.

Generally speaking, Amish quilts are characterized by bold, solid colors pieced in stark, geometric shapes and lovingly quilted with tiny stitches. Amish quilts hold a special place in the quilting world, but little is known about the traditions behind them.

Today's Old Order Amish still shun photographs of themselves as being prideful, but the women were willing to talk to Rachel about the part quilts play in their daily lives. She is well-known among Amish quilters. Her work as a quilt historian provides a rare opportunity to understand and appreciate the culture behind the quilts.

Amish quiltmakers' lives have changed little from their foremothers. They go to quilting bees where they learn about who's dating, who's have a baby, who's moving. Little girls who have not mastered their stitches help prepare the meal for the quilters. Quilting is a sharing time for the women, as mothers and daughters work together. As one woman says, "We had a lot of precious moments sitting together quilting."

The Amish community's sense of belonging nurtures the practice of quiltmaking, explains Rachel Pellman, in her book *Treasury of Amish Quilts:*

- The Amish, as a community, continue to practice a strong work ethic—adults spend little time in non-productive activities.
- Quality of work is as important as the quantity of work. Amish respect a job well done.
- "Art for art's sake" is a little understood concept within the teaching of the Amish. The creative spirit is not stifled, but the end result of a creative endeavor must have purpose.
- Quilting reinforces the social fabric of the Amish community.
- Quilts are an acceptable way to show appreciation and caring within the community.

Today, the marketing of Amish quilts has impacted materials used—printed fabric is starting to appear in quilts for sale.

Known for their simple, unadorned lifestyle, the Amish use surprisingly vivid colors in their quilt work. —JJ

Behind the Seams

AMERICAN QUILTER

Dianne S. Hire, of Northport, Maine, is a free spirit who has quilting on her mind constantly. "I have to quilt one way or another all the time," she says. Today, *American Quilter* joins Dianne at her home, where quilting, gardens, family, friends, and faith make up the elements of her daily life.

Her quilts are whimsical, playful creations in vibrant colors and unusual fabric combinations. Her style is improvisational. "It has no rules to it," she says. "I like to break rules." Sometimes, she begins a quilt with a watercolor mock-up. At other times, she takes pieces from her scrap basket and just starts putting them together. However she arrives at her magnificent designs, she has a box full of awards to show for it, and her work hangs in exhibitions all over the world.

One of her favorite ways to quilt is to "play"—yes, play! "Play is a valuable teacher," she smiles. "Play stretches us to test the edges between reality and fantasy, between linear and oblique ways of thinking. Play finds joy in the process rather than than in the product. Play has the potential for discovering order in the madness of a sometimes chaotic world." So Dianne plays.

As a teacher and lecturer, Dianne invites quilters of all skill levels to her playground. Taking one of her classes is a liberating experience. "I found freedom in quilting," says one student after the class.

Dianne is also consumed by her gardens, creating a quilt of a different sort. "This is my summer piecing," she says. With husband, Terry, Dianne is passionate about their extensive gardens and stone walls. Carefully, she selects stone to build walls, with the same mind-set she uses to select fabric for her quilts.

"I'm driven to create," explains Dianne. Gardens, home and, of course, quilts are her playgrounds.

Dianne was a model in college and became a couture dress buyer. She believes that this experience helped teach her good design. "I learned good design. I was surrounded by good design," she says.

Today, Dianne's art quilts are exhibited around the world. Husband Terry says that, even if she created a quilt a day, she would never reach a point where she will have satisfied her need to create.

She is joined in her love of quilting by her husband, who is an artist and designer in his own right,. He loves to needlepoint interpretations of quilts.

Within the English tradition, the more proper name for this style might be "framed quilts" in reference to the sequence of framing borders used in their construction. However, the term "medallion" has settled into our contemporary quilt vernacular. A quilt's center may be pieced, appliquéd, *broderie perse,* or a single commemorative textile.

In this episode, Bettina shows how to make and use cardboard templates and prepare the fabric pieces for piecing. "Preparation is important in any project,' she stresses, "but with hand piecing, you're relying on the precision of the pieces and the skill of your hands, so you don't want to compromise those things by being careless." Today, Bettina shows us the proper way to construct a Mariner's Compass. Many think that this a particularly difficult block to

Bettina Havig generously presented me with the beautiful star block she created for this Savvy Quilter segment. —JJ

SAVVY QUILTER

Bettina Havig of Columbia, Missouri, joins the show as this week's Savvy Quilter. She is a woman of many passions—teacher, author, historian, judge, and consultant. She has immersed herself in quilting since the 1970s. Today, she is known for her fine hand piecing and her love for the traditions of English medallion quilts.

perfect. Bettina advises us to break down the elements of the block and begin hand piecing from the corners, moving toward the center. Successful Mariner's Compass blocks begin with good planning, accurate templates, precision cutting, and building the block from the corners in.

QUILT OF THE WEEK

AMERICAN STILL LIFE (80" x 80") by Sandra Leichner of Albany, Oregon, is our quilt of the week. Sandra is heavily influenced by the events around her, and she tries to tell a story with her quilts. Sandra says that this is her 9/11 quilt, and during the process of making it, we had the Columbia disaster and the start of the Iraqi war. "This quilt conveys a story of the American people, their strength, and enduring spirit in a difficult time in this country's history," she explains.

The quilt contains a lot of stuffed appliqué, including twenty-five berries. She also used needle weaving in her embellishment. For her next project, Sandra wants to make another traditionally based quilt with even more embellishment.

Sandra believes it is her love of gardens and flowers that is prevalent in her art. As a native Oregonian, she is surrounded by lush gardens, magnificent rain forests, and the coast. These influences are reflected in her quilts.

"It is my kids who are responsible for my discovery of quilting," Sandra says. She had decided to make a baby blanket but didn't have the slightest clue how. So, her first quilt was tied and constructed without regard to matching points or knowing how to bind it. Now, when someone remarks that Sanda Leichner has "never made a bad quilt," she just laughs and pulls out that first baby quilt. Of course, today, Sandra's work is highly revered for its excellence.

This magnificent tribute to America gives the illusion of a leather background and is one of my husband's favorites.
— JJ

Episode Guide

EPISODE ONE
American Quilter: Caryl Bryer Fallert, Illinois
Savvy Quilter: Sue Nickels, Michigan
Quilt of the Week: Shirley Kelly, New York
Quiltscapes: Quilters Guild of Indianapolis, Indiana
Pieceful Quilter: Norton House, Vermont

EPISODE TWO
American Quilter: Karen Kay Buckley, Pennsylvania
Savvy Quilter: Joan Shay, Massachusetts
Quilt of the Week: John Flynn, Montana
Quiltscapes: Robert Cargo African-American Quilt
    Collection, Alabama
Pieceful Quilter: Making Fabric, Cranston Print Works,
    Massachusetts

EPISODE THREE
American Quilter: Gerald E. Roy, New Hampshire
Savvy Quilter: Bethany S. Reynolds, Maine
Quilt of the Week: Linda Carlson, Missouri
Quiltscapes: Behind the Scenes of American Quilter:
    Helen Squire
Pieceful Quilter: Bobbin Lace Demonstration, Kentucky

EPISODE FOUR
American Quilter: Georgia Bonesteel, North Carolina
Savvy Quilter: Fran Morgan, Texas
Quilt of the Week: Sue Gilgen, Wisconsin
Quiltscapes: Heritage Museum Esprit Collection, Pennsylvania
Pieceful Quilter: Making Thread, Robison-Anton Thread
    Company, Pennsylvania

EPISODE FIVE
American Quilter: Libby Lehman, Texas
Savvy Quilter: Karen Combs, Tennessee
Quilt of the Week: Aie Rossmann, Canada
Quiltscapes: Hopi Native American Quilts, Arizona
Pieceful Quilter: Making Batting, Hobbs Bonded Fibers,
    Texas

EPISODE SIX
American Quilter: Jennifer Chiaverini, Wisconsin
Savvy Quilter: Bonnie K. Browning, Kentucky
Quilt of the Week: Historical Kits, Nebraska
Quiltscapes: A Day in the Life of a Show Director:
    Bonnie K. Browning
Pieceful Quilter: Antique Quilt Dealer, Laura Fisher, New York

EPISODE SEVEN

American Quilter: Fraser Smith, Florida
Savvy Quilter: Linda M. Poole, Pennsylvania
Quilt of the Week: Diane Gaudynski, Wisconsin
Quiltscapes: Museum of American Quilter's Society, Kentucky
Pieceful Quilter: Quilt Studio, Gerald E. Roy, New Hampshire

EPISODE EIGHT

American Quilter: Quilters on the Road, Wisconsin
Savvy Quilter: Sally Terry, Kentucky
Quilt of the Week: Gail Garber, New Mexico
Quiltscapes: Quilts on Main Festival, Missouri
Pieceful Quilter: Hand Quilting with Virginia "Rusty" Hedrick, Tennessee

EPISODE NINE

American Quilter: Arturo Sandoval, Kentucky
Savvy Quilter: Bobbie A. Aug, Colorado
Quilt of the Week: Nancy S. Brown, California
Quiltscapes: AQS Quilt Exposition, Tennessee
Pieceful Quilter: Tour Through Amish Country, Pennsylvania

EPISODE TEN

American Quilter: Pat Campbell, Texas
Savvy Quilter: Suzanne Marshall, Missouri
Quilt of the Week: Bill Lyle, Illinois
Quiltscapes: Kansas State Fair, Kansas
Pieceful Quilter: Antique Quilt Bed Turning, Tennessee

EPISODE ELEVEN

American Quilter: Anita Shackelford, Ohio
Savvy Quilter: Debbie Bowles, Minnesota
Quilt of the Week: Sue Nickels and Pat Holly, Michigan
Quiltscapes: University of Nebraska International Quilt Study Center, Nebraska
Pieceful Quilter: Long-Arm Quilting, Gammill Quilting Systems, Tennessee

EPISODE TWELVE

American Quilter: Hollis Chatelain, North Carolina
Savvy Quilter: Pat Yamin, New York
Quilt of the Week: Martha Nordstrand, California
Quiltscapes: Rebecca Barker's Quiltscape Paintings, Ohio
Pieceful Quilter: Hand Piecing, Bettina Havig, Missouri

EPISODE THIRTEEN

American Quilter: Dianne S. Hire, Maine
Savvy Quilter: Bettina Havig, Missouri
Quilt of the Week: Sandra Leichner, Oregon
Quiltscapes: Rachel Pellman, Amish Interviews, Pennsylvania
Pieceful Quilter: Mary Ghormley's Miniature Quilts, Nebraska

AMERICAN Quilter MAGAZINE

• Profiles and interviews with today's finest celebrity quiltmakers.

• Well-written articles, beautiful color photography, and award-winning quilts.

FREE with Membership in American Quilter's Society

Spring Summer Fall Ultimate Projects Winter

American Quilter TELEVISION

• Focuses on the passions, people, community, art, and function of this unique lifestyle.

• In-depth interviews, rich visuals, and compelling character-driven storytelling.

DVD Series Buy one or the entire set

American Quilter Series — DVD — HOSTED BY Jeanna Juleson — copyright© American Quilter's Society — www.AmericanQuilter.com — Episode One Two Three

American Quilter Series — Episode Four Five Six

American Quilter Series — Episode Seven Eight Nine

American Quilter Series — Episode Ten Eleven Twelve·Thirteen

For more information contact

www.AmericanQuilter.com
1-800-626-5420